From Poetry to Pickles

The Reflections and Original Recipes
Of The Pickle Queen

By Shirley Stimpert

Published by:
Hearth and Home Publishing

From Poetry to Pickles
By Shirley Stimpert

Copyright © 2001
Shirley Stimpert
All Rights Reserved

ISBN: 0-9706672-05
LCCN: 00-93694

Published by Hearth and Home Publishing
12989 Windy Road • Bucklin, KS 67834
316-826-3491

Cover Photo by Garrett McClure as featured in USA Today.

To order additional copies of this book or information on forthcoming books by this author, call 316-826-3491 or write to address of Hearth and Home Publishing. Order forms can be found in the back of the book.

Printed in the U.S.A. by Morris Publishing
3212 East Hwy. 30 • Kearney, NE 68847
800-650-7888

Table of Contents

The Story – How it Began 12
It Wasn't Easy 14
Bipartisan Pickles with a Personality 17
The Toast 18
From a Country Heart 19
Good Food! Good Fun! 20
Summer Sensation 21
    A Country Fourth of July 22
Fourth of July Salad 23
    Hearth-side Fun 24
Picnic Poppers 25
Our Customers Tell Us 27
All the Young'uns 28
Pickled Young'uns 29
    Veggies-n-Popcorn 29
Putting Up Time 30
Pickled Beets 31
    Pickled Eggs in Beet Syrup 31
Hope And A Prayer 32
Asparagus Nubbins 33
    Small Thrills 34
Spring Has Sprung Salad 35
Burnished Splendor 36
Pickled Brussel Sprouts 37
    Rappin' Brussel Sprouts 39
Scottish Country Wedding 41
Poem – Legacy 43
Pickles and Pods 45
    Home Again 46
A Simple Country Supper 47
Cherry Picking Time 48
Celestial Cherries 49
Daffodils and Butterflies 51
Poem – Butter Churns and Daisies 53

Essay – The Tulip is Only a Season 55
Perky Pineapple 57
   First Grandchild 58
   Perky Pineapple Pork 59
Tough Love 60
Pickled Okra 61
   Summer Nights 62
Summertime Supper Salad 63
Peck of Pickled Peppers 65
   Miss Piggy and Her Piglets 66
Perky Peppered Pork 67
Pickled Jalapenos 69
   The "Triple S" Sandwich 71
Ravishing Red Peppers 73
Autumn Holdouts 74
Pickled Onions 75
The Note 76
Sweet Corn Relish 77
   Fruit of the Womb 78
Cowboy Casserole 79
   Corny Pasta Salad 81
   The Corn Belt Special 81
Calico Beans 83
   Memories of the Heart 84
Calico Chili 85
   Calico Taco Salad 87
Southern Heritage 88
Dilly Green Southwest Tomatoes 89
   Grilled Southwest Salad 91
Honey – D – Green Tomatoes 93
   Dinner Bell 95
Honeyed Swiss Chicken 95
Pickled Garlic 97
   Ritzy Garlic 99
   Garlic Taters 99
Bread and Butter Pickles 101
   The Monday Night Special 103
Racy Raspberries 105

Kansas Buttermilk Pie with Racy Raspberries	106
Blueberry Bash	109
A Heartland Christmas	110
Dad's Christmas Brunch Pancakes	111
The Christmas Gift	113
Olives & Eve	117
Gathering the Eggs	118
Eve's Scalloped Chicken	119
Sweet Pickle Relish	121
Garden Potato Salad	123
A Traditional Thanksgiving	125
Turkey Salad Sandwiches	125
Pickled Asparagus	126
The Smell of Wood Smoke	127
Asparagus Pork Rollups with Herb Butter	127
Sweet Summer Medley	129
Pork Cutlet Sandwiches	129
Food Is An Art	130
Pickled Carrots	131
Pickled Carrot Pinwheels	131
Sweet Red Relish	133
Tuesday's Tuna Teasers	133
Marvelous Mandarin Oranges	135
Orange and Chicken Stir-fry	137
Brazen Fruit Vinegarettes	139
In Conclusion	141
Order Pages	143

Dear Readers, Fans and Pickle Lovers,

My journey from nationally published writer and poetry prizewinner to Pickle Queen was fast, fun, fulfilling, always frantic and never boring! In response to you, my customers, (and often my friends) I'll pause to reflect and share my memories, observations and of course the recipes you've asked for for so long - the recipes for our famous Pickle Cottage pickled products. They are the only pickles to ever be featured in The Wall Street Journal.

To all of you, this book is written with love and a grateful heart. I'll miss you! I'm thankful for your loyalty and support, but most of all for you friendship.

Many of you have said, "What will we do without you?" This book is my gift of love back to you, as you will now be able to pack your own pickles with our famous recipes. Think of us when you do and strive for the simpler lifestyle our products represent. Good memories are gifts given eternally. Thank you for sharing them with me.

God has blessed Barry and me to be able to retire to our beautiful family farm, where we live off of the land with a passion and a simplicity rarely experienced in this age.

We share our fruitful land with our sons and their families. We are amused to hear comments such as, "You live a storybook life, you remind me of the Waltons." I have much to return home to.

Like an exotic traveler, my experiences have been heady, thrilling, challenging and at times almost unbelievable. From humble country beginnings, I've been thrust into national prominence, met heads of state and movie stars, been featured in over 200 publications and been on both television and radio. I've been invited as a guest on several well-known television talk shows. I've been offered contracts for modeling, movies and buy-outs. National publishing companies have been discussing a book contract since 1996.

The success of our company and the popularity of our products have resulted in our pickles being sold in all fifty states as well as overseas in such famous stores as Herrod's of London, Pier I Imports, Bloomingdale's, Cracker Barrel, Dean & Deluca, Harry & David, Silver Dollar City, Dollywood, QVC and many others.

Like all thrilling novels, this one has a final chapter and with it I will close this portion of my life. Each new dawn brings blank pages of my next novel, one of a simple, back to basics lifestyle filled with soul-satisfying moments, love and laughter, hard work that clears the mind and enriches the body and of course the good food that raising and preparing your own brings.

Perhaps you wonder why I would leave such an exciting and successful lifestyle for one of simplicity. Success wears many faces and appears to us in different ways at each phase of our lives. Thus we grow and mature and hopefully in the end are better for the composite of them.

I sense my final novel shall be my best, as I return home to the land I love and the family that's one with me. It's true, Scarlett does return home to Tara and I must go home to Heartland.

In the future I will publish a series of books on our country lifestyle, filled with old-fashioned wisdom and country moments, additional cookbooks, how-to books, poetry and reflections of country living. Order forms are included in the back of the book.

Wishing all of you true joy, love and laughter. May all of your pickles be good ones!

Always,
Shirley Stimpert
The Pickle Queen

To You -
For Giving of Yourselves

To Barry – My husband, my love, my friend – always there, always strong, my balance, we did it together! Thank you for a marriage truly 'made in heaven.'

To my son Trent – Thank you. Remember our sleepless nights and hot days. You gave of yourself for the dream - to help birth the company, in long hot hours, through thick and thin, a sacrifice of love from beginning to end. I love you!

To my son Marc – Thank you for your legal advice, your undying love and loyalty. You have always believed in your Mom and encouraged my will to succeed. We write poetry together in our hearts, my son! Love lives forever!

To my son Jared – Thank you for standing at our side to build the farm and the company. Through your eyes, I see butterflies in whole new ways and experience love in new dimensions. You enrich my spirit and my soul prospers in your love. Thank you for the gift of you!

To my son Trevor – Thank you for staying to help – even when your talents pulled you in other directions. Sometimes, at the end of a stressful day, your smile and soft eyes can light up my path again, and your sensitive heart expands my vision. May we always plant trees together, now and in the age to come!

To my daughter Shandlla – Thank you for being the best shipping manager and friend and now the daughter I never had and letting me be the mother you never had. You're a gift from God, beautiful both on the inside and the outside.

To my daughter Rebecca – Thank you for so many blessings – first of all for helping me put this book into print. For your help in the cannery and on the computer, and especially for our little Abby and the new grandbaby coming soon! I'll always remember the encouraging note you faxed to us during the days of "raspberry river." Thanks honey! You too are a special gift.

To my daughter Gretchen – You're the newest daughter of mine. Already I have much to thank you for. Thank you for loving Marc and all of us. It really blesses us! Also, thanks for your sweet offer to type my books for free. Your loyalty and love are a gift from God.

To my sister Judy Joy – You were by my side the day I named the Pickle Cottage and you were my first employee. Your constant love and friendship make you a joy, a part of our family and the sister I never had. God sent you to us. I thank Him and you!

To my cat Spiggs – Thank you. You're the three-legged love of my life! Thanks for the 'purr-fect' friendship.

To my friend Chris – Thanks for long, hot days, stress management, being loyal at difficult times and 'saving my bacon' more than once! We appreciated you!

To my friend Sue – "The Prep Queen" Thank you for honesty, loyalty and true caring for our family. Good work!

The Story - How It Began

"It Was An Accident"

People ask me almost daily, "How did you get started in this?" Others who know the story often remark, "Your story reminds me of that movie, 'Baby Boom'." Yes, it is very similar.

It all began when I inherited my family farm and moved there. My husband was teaching at the time and I was a free-lance writer working on assignment with seven national magazines. We loved our farm and have always had a passion for a back to basics, living off the land lifestyle.

We began to work towards our ultimate goal of total self-sufficiency on our farm. In the beginning, it was obvious that the income did not match the needs, so I began to supplement our income with sales of fresh produce and pickles at a small local Farmer's Market.

There was a state organized promotion at the time and the buyer from Bloomingdale's got some of my pickles. I will never forget that day! I was walking through the house when the phone rang. "You're serious – Bloomingdale's? You love my pickles? You'll take all that I can send? Wow!" Barry found me dancing on the ceiling after that first BIG order.

Glitz comes naturally to some of us, but experience brings sophistication. Our first order shipped was very inexperienced as we struggled to get on top of a wave that was fast carrying us into a sea of new experiences.

From that first big order, the tide continued to rise as famous stores and famous people began to clamor for our pickles. We could not even keep up with the demand. We often spent 20-hour days and even one 23-hour day, in efforts to meet our demands.

Reporters, photographers and journalists began haunting my haven. In all, we were featured in over 200 publications, including The Wall Street Journal and USA Today. I have appeared multiple times on TV and radio. We've been filmed live on location at our

Heartland Farm twice, once where Barry, my husband, gave me his now famous 'Rhett and Scarlett' kiss. (I received more calls on the kiss than on the pickles the next day!) I've also been featured live on QVC, and have been offered television modeling work – all because of pickles!

'Pickle Queen Turns Farm Fare Into Fancy City Treats,' the headline in The Wall Street Journal confirmed my new title, as did the caricature of me in royal attire and crown in the same feature. Just months later, in celebration of National Pickle Week, USA Today ran the following clip, 'Pickle Queen Celebrates National Pickle Week!' Just a thought, vinegar is great for cleaning crowns!

These were just two of many headlines confirming my new title. When I returned to my former, simple country lifestyle, the headlines read, 'Pickle Queen Goes Back to the Basics.' Whether in the city or in the country, once a Pickle Queen, always a Pickle Queen!

The farm raised, hand-packed beauty and taste of our pickles in conjunction with our way of living brought raves. The die was cast, my fate was sealed, The Pickle Queen was born. Some of life's best moments are accidents!

It Wasn't Easy

Sometimes it's hard to see the pain behind the gain. I remember a time, early in the company, before all my employees arrived to help out. It was just our family packing thousands and thousands of jars in our first tiny cannery.

We had just been awarded our first big contract, 18,000 jars! The buyer, knowing we were new to the whole national gourmet scene, was impressed with both me and my products, yet unsure of my ability to produce the contract in the specified time frame necessary. Remember, all our pickles are hand-packed. In order to finalize the contract, we had to ship at an exact date, give or take a few days. If we couldn't perform, the contract would be off and I'd be left literally 'holding the note.'

The buyer, who represented a huge international company and whom I came to consider a personal friend, was professional, yet compassionate. She asked me before awarding me the contract if I thought I could really do it. I replied, "No, I don't think I can do it. I KNOW I can do it!" She later confided, "That statement and your confidence is the main reason I gave you the contract." We continued a close business relationship for most of my career in The Pickle Cottage.

Now I had the contract in hand. 'The fat was in the fire,' so to speak. I'm a firm believer that, God-willing, I can do almost anything I set my mind to do!

We calculated the number of units we would have to can each day and even translated that into units per hour. My family was with me. We would do what we said we could do – no matter what!

For the next weeks, I canned, ate a little (standing because I couldn't take time to sit down) drank gallons of Coke to brace me, suffered terrible heat and humidity, slept as little as 1 to 4 hours every 24 hours and rarely saw the inside of my home. Our boys began to joke, upon my infrequent trips to the house, "Could that be our mom? It kind of looks like Mom."

I wasn't alone. Barry, Judy and our precious sons shared my pain. Our progress was almost right on course, we were only a little behind our deadline. The last week before ship date saw the final adrenalin rush! Everyone shifted into overdrive!

The last day, or should I say, the night and day of canning allowed us no margin of error. Only perfection would be enough. Barry and Judy never left my side. And the boys, still young then, insisted on loving me and our dream, by staying up almost all night to help. Trent and I had to keep waking each other up. I fell asleep once, on my feet, with a knife in my hand!

Jared, my youngest, was our little trooper. He went to bring more produce to the cannery. It seemed like forever and he still wasn't back. I went to check on him and found him asleep in the yard, the raw produce beside him. That's a night we remember with laughter and pain. It was one moment in time – and we did it together. We knew we were the best we could be and all the naysayers had to 'eat crow!' It felt good. It felt right. We had pushed ourselves to the brink, like a test pilot with a hot new airplane, and we didn't crash. Instead we soared with the eagles!

Bipartisan Pickles With A Personality

All of the heads of state eat Pickle Cottage pickles or they eat no pickles at all. (Or at least we hoped so!)

Actually, our famous line of pickles have been enjoyed by notables such as Senator Bob Dole, who loves our Pickles & Pods, and used our gift pack for the V.I.P. press corps when he announced his bid for the Presidency of the United States.

Then there was the famous Kansas Buttermilk Pie with Racy Raspberry topping which enjoyed favor at the Earls Court in London, England.

We have also made a gift pack for the State Department, which was given to Boris Yeltsin when he visited our nation.

In addition, our pickles were sampled by international diplomats arriving from their respective embassies at Dean & Deluca in Washington, D.C. Of course, I wore my popular stars and stripes dress and found myself being saluted and kisses thrown at me. Maybe the bodyguard they provided was a good idea after all!

Our pickles have graced the tables for Secret Service events. I also personally served them in the Governor's mansion in Topeka, Kansas. They were even featured at some Presidential Roundtable get-togethers.

We were also honored to host the pre-election day dinner in our home on Heartland Farm for our now U.S. Senator Pat Roberts and his family. Pickles were popular that evening also.

U.S. Senator Sam Brownback, in his former position in our Kansas Agricultural Department, praised and displayed our line of value-added pickles on television.

For these honors and joys you have given me, Gentlemen and Ladies, I salute you back!

"The Toast - His Grace"

While attending a party in Dallas, Texas to honor the grand opening of a rather large and very famous chain of stores, the leading CEO of the company looked straight at me and proclaimed the following toast and blessing over me: "To the lady with natural glitz; no sooner do you speak it, than it reaches the Father's ears."

Since I had not had a chance to share my close relationship to God with him yet, I felt my spirit electrify with the truth of his pronouncement.

It's God that grants us the grace to walk out our callings. It's my faith in Him and our relationship of love that gave me – gave all of us – the strength and the vision to do what we did. His constant presence in our lives is the foundation of all we are and all we do. I shall give Him the glory forever and acknowledge Him before men so that Jesus might acknowledge me before His Father.

We are one family united in love, for God is love and our motto is 'love never fails'!

I thank Him for my last life novel and pray for His will to be done in my next one. Glory be to God.

"From a Country Heart"

I stand surrounded by the beauty of my bounty. Before me, in my storage room, are rows of colorful mason jars filled with natural foods that we raised or grew, fished or searched for. There they stand, a testimony to faith in a seed, love of the land, hard work that toughens us - yet softens us, and perhaps most of all to creativity and love, that which is best in us!

I also realize I'm living a life that few have lived today in our new high-tech world. I realize once more why so many of you marvel at my lifestyle and long to imitate it. For you, my friends, this next section: 'Good Food! Good Fun!' gives you a chance, no matter how large or small, to feel the way I feel right now – basking in my canned bounty – knowing I grew it, canned it and will not go hungry when cold winds come.

"Good Food! Good Fun!"

"Is it to eat or to look at?" People often ask this question. "It's too beautiful to open, but too good not to." Summer Sensation, the Pickle Queen's own creation, has won food art awards for it's outstanding, colorful beauty. Yet this perky, fresh taste is relished by all.

Known as my 'signature product' this mix of summer's best vegetables fresh from our gardens (or yours) pickled with sprigs of aromatic dill weed, bring back memories of lazy Sunday summer afternoons fishing on the dock at our version of Golden Pond when all the family's home.

Summer Sensation

Our colorful garden mixture of summer's best vegetables is pure poetry in a jar! Pickled in our spicy dilled brine, the crisp pickles delight all the senses. Let their country signature accent your kitchen.

Makes about 12 pints
Brine: Mix and bring to a boil:
      1 gallon water (best without chlorine)
      1/2 gallon white vinegar (5% acidity)
      1 1/8 cups pickling salt (do not use table salt)
Wash and sterilize jars and lids.
Spices per jar:
      Pint: 1/4 teaspoon mustard seed
      Quart: 1/2 teaspoon mustard seed
      1/2 Gallon: 1 teaspoon mustard seed

Wash the following young vegetables in equal amounts: Cauliflower (broken apart), baby carrots, yellow summer squash, baby or young pickling cucumbers, fresh garlic cloves (several per jar), hot red peppers (1 per pint jar), and tender young green dill weed (2 sprigs per pint jar).

Cold-pack the vegetables and dill weed in an artistic arrangement in your sterilized jars. Pack tightly to avoid floating of vegetables. Fill to lower ring of jars.

Pour boiling brine into jars, leaving 1/4" to 1/8" headspace at the top of your jars. Cap the jars and process in a boiling water bath for 12 minutes for pints, 16 minutes for quarts and 21 minutes for 1/2 gallon jars.

Remove and let cool till sealed. Check all jars for proper seal. If not sealed, reprocess at full times or refrigerate and enjoy soon!

Summer Sensation Uses and Suggestions::

Summer Sensation is sensational in all fresh vegetable salads and is glorious on a relish tray. Also, try our recipe for Picnic Poppers and the unique Fourth of July Salad our family loves. May all your Summers be Sensational!

"A Country Fourth of July"

In the country, we who live by the heartbeat of the seasons view July 4th as the peak of summer's best. Everything before then in early summer builds to that time and the remainder of late summer slowly descends into the warmth of the Cicada's rhythmic whine.

Our family loves July 4th and we always celebrate with a big country party. Fireworks, good food, family and friends, romantic night skies – of these things memories are made.

Serve this salad and it's July in January.

Fourth of July Salad

Makes a large family-sized bowl
1 head Romaine lettuce
1 small bunch radishes
1 bunch red-leaf lettuce
1 bunch green-leaf lettuce
1 large bag spinach leaves
1 red onion (diced)
8 garden ripened tomatoes
a few sprigs cilantro
a few sprigs dill weed
a few sprigs parsley
1 pint drained Summer Sensation pickles - cut into bite size pieces

Toss all vegetables and pickles together in very large salad bowl. Dress with reserved Summer Sensation brine mixed with olive oil and Italian seasonings. Finish dressing with oil and vinegar dressing of your choice.

Note: Any dressing can be used, and is good.

Hearth-side Fun

Our beautiful old family farmhouse at Heartland features a twelve-foot-wide open hearth walk-in fireplace, complete with a separate brick bake oven and large crane.

As the leaves begin to turn to autumn's glory and the night's twilight chill send us from field to hearthside earlier - the fireplace once again mesmerizes the family and becomes the center of the home for the duration of the winter until spring breaks the spell of the cold time.

Indoor hearthside picnics can be spontaneous family fun or an unusual get-together for friends. Serve our Picnic Poppers – they'll be the hit of the party!

Picnic Poppers

Cut up bite-size serving pieces of mixed Summer Sensation pickled vegetables. Dip each piece in batter and deep fry until crisp.

Golden Puff Batter
1 cup flour
1 tablespoon sugar
1 1/2 teaspoon baking powder
1/2 teaspoon salt
1/2 teaspoon chili powder
2 eggs beaten
1/3 cup milk
1 Tablespoon vegetable oil

Sift flour, sugar, baking powder, salt and chili powder into a small bowl. Add eggs, milk and vegetable oil. Stir until smooth. Batter can be prepared ahead of time and stored in a covered container in refrigerator. If batter becomes too thick, stir in 1 tablespoon cold milk.

Our Customers Tell Us ...

We would often get calls or hear stories from our women customers similar to the ones printed here. Summer Sensation, as well as many of our other pickled vegetables and fruits, have won art awards and are often used for decorative purposes.

Interior designers nationwide have used our products to glorious advantage. We have even been asked if our products are real or artificial. Customers remarking, "It's so perfect, so pretty, I didn't think it was real. Can I really eat it?" Yes you can. But enjoy the country class the colorful mixes bring to your décor also.

Another customer called to say: "I came home and he was eating my pickles and watching football. I'm so angry! He told me that he thought it was food. I told him it was…but it wasn't!" Calming down a little, she continued, "Well, at least he said I can order several more half-gallon jars."

A regular customer of ours, desperate to keep her hubby's wandering hands out of her designer pickles, went so far as to threaten to put something in the jar to kill him if he ate them again. We recommend that you purchase or make extras to enjoy looking at and eating. Remember the old adage, "A good man is hard to find."

All the Young'uns...

I was in our commercial cannery kitchens, in the process of canning Pickled Young'uns when the phone rang. I picked up answering with my customary, "The Pickle Cottage, may I help you?" The customer seemed pleased to be speaking to me personally and asked what I was doing. In response I said, "I'm canning Young'uns." After an awkward silence, the question was posed, "They can't be that bad can they?" You'll find our Young'uns are always good. They're so pretty that Pier 1 Imports featured them in a Good Housekeeping Christmas advertisement.

Another one of the Pickle Queen's original recipes, this striped mix of orange, yellow and green vegetable strips is glorious on a snack or relish platter.

Our Young'uns were born when Alan Palmer, buyer for the famous Bloomingdale's, left the following request on my answering machine: "Hey, Doll. How about creating a beautiful striped pickle of young vegetables for me? You've got twelve hours!"

Trevor, our then young son, had the honor of naming the now famous Young'uns. He remembers the time when he was with me at one of our larger stores. He mentioned to a customer that was purchasing a jar of Young'uns that he had named them Young'uns originally and his family owned the company. The customer laughed and replied, "Sure you did kid."

All of the Young'uns, both pickles and children have turned out well at Heartland.

Pickled Young'uns Recipe

Makes brine for 20 pints
Brine:
> 12 cups water
> 4 cups white vinegar (5% acidity)
> 1/2 cup pickling salt

Spices per jar:
> 1/2 teaspoon dill seed
> 1/2 teaspoon pickling spice
> 1/8 teaspoon minced garlic

Wash equal amounts of yellow summer squash and zucchini. Cut to fit the length of you pint mason jars allowing for 1/4" headspace. Cut squash into long wedges. Cut an amount of peeled carrots to equal the amount of total yellow and green summer squash. Wedge it. Put spices in the bottom of canning jars. Cold pack the yellow, green and orange strips into jar in an upright position and alternating colors evenly.

Bring brine to a boil. Pour hot into packed jars. Wipe mouth of jars with sterile cloth. Cap jars and process in boiling water bath for 12 minutes. Cool and let seal. Check for seals after jars are cool.

Pickled Young'uns Uses and Suggestions:

Great for the holidays on relish trays – colorful and tasty. Use for drink stirrers for vegetable juices and cocktails. They're also great in salads. Pretty in your cabinet too!

Veggies-n-Popcorn

Along with a family sized bowl of hot buttered popcorn, serve a side platter of Young'uns arranged as pinwheels on a festive tray. Our style of farm living leaves little time for loafing! When we manage to make time for television or a movie, we like to add to the fun with snacks. What's the Pickle Queen's favorite TV series? It's "Little House on the Prairie." Actually, I live my own series, "Big House on the Prairie." It's true – fact is far more interesting that fiction.

Putting Up Time

Country living, so simple yet so complex, has a pattern and a rhythm which cannot be ignored if we truly wish to receive our provision from our surroundings. It's autumn. 'Putting up time' as we think of it, has come. The sounds of Canadian Geese overhead mark the days. The crisp crackling of firewood spitting comforts the heart, knowing the cozy hearth days lie just ahead.

No other smell, wafting from our country kitchen during one of these bittersweet days, pronounces the bounty that is autumn more than old-fashioned Pickled Beets. Earthy, spicy, rich with vibrant color, they link us once more to the past.

Generations of country women have 'put up' maroon jars of beets with this turn-of-the-century recipe, which is a family heirloom recipe on my husband's side. Healthy, hardy, wholesome, now you can make and enjoy Pickled Beets like those Grandma used to make.

Pickled Beets

Approximately 50 pounds raw, young beets. Cook beets in boiling water until tender and skins slip off easily, usually about one or two hours. Dip beets into cold water and drain. Peel and wedge or slice. Small beets can be left whole.

Make a syrup of the following:
1 1/2 gallons vinegar (white or cider) 5% acidity
1 1/2 gallons water
    1 1/2 gallons sugar (about 24 cups)
    1 1/2 cups lemon juice
    5 Tablespoons ground cinnamon
    5 Tablespoons ground cloves
    5 Tablespoons ground allspice

Bring syrup and beet mixture almost to a boil (about 15 to 20 minutes). Pack beets hot into clean mason jars. Cover with hot syrup, leaving 1/4" headspace at the top of jars. Process in a boiling water bath for 7 minutes. Remove and cool. Check for proper seals.

Pickled Beets Uses and Suggestions:
Another old German favorite from the 'seven sweet and seven sours' group, Pickled Beets go great with any traditional fare. Beet lovers eat them right out of the jar.

Many of the old-fashioned methods of preserving food are no more than memories or dusty scraps of recipes in long forgotten trunks. Eggs, a staple of pioneer life, were often preserved in waterglass in absence of refrigeration. Another old favorite was Pickled Eggs. The recipe below is from a different era.

Pickled Eggs in Beet Syrup
Boil desired amount of eggs until hard-boiled. Let cool a little. Bring the leftover Pickled Beet sweet syrup to a boil. Add the peeled, hard-boiled eggs (left whole) to the hot syrup. Allow the eggs to sit in the refrigerator for at least 3 – 4 days. Enjoy! The eggs turn a pretty burgundy and are beautiful on top of salads.

Hope And A Prayer

Country thriftiness, once admired by our society, is now sadly often scorned. Frugal country homemakers used to use up every scrap and morsel, make do and improvise when needed. They raised their families on little more than hope and a prayer. Yet the memories of their offspring often reflect childhoods filled with comfort, love and lack of want.

More does not always equal better and is sometimes less. Our often lazy, throw-away society of today has little respect for the old country philosophy, 'waste not, want not.'

We often set our own traps and are so surprised to "wake up in the middle of the day," as the country pop hit goes, and find ourselves in them.

This recipe, Asparagus Nubbins, was born out of my pioneer heritage of just such frugality. After cutting my asparagus tips just the right lengths for my mason jars, I needed a use for the remainder of the asparagus stalks. Thus was conceived the Nubbins. This product is multi-talented. Everyone loves them!

Asparagus Nubbins

Makes about 15 pints

10 pounds diced or sliced asparagus ends. (does not include tender tip)

2 pounds peeled and sliced carrots

1/2 can red pimento pepper

Mix the above ingredients together evenly in a separate container. Pack into mason pint jars, leaving 1/4" headspace.

Brine:

    4 cups white vinegar (5% acidity)

    12 cups water

    3/4 cup pickling salt

Bring the brine mixture to a boil and pour hot into packed jars, leaving 1/4" headspace. Cap and process in boiling water bath for 12 minutes. Cool and check for seal.

Asparagus Nubbins Uses and Suggestions:

Excellent added to all salads; fruit vegetable, potato, and pasta. Good lightly sautéed or grilled as a side dish.

Small Thrills

It helps to cultivate a healthy sense of humor in the country. It really evens things out. I had to chuckle when one of our daughter-in-laws went racing to relieve the mailbox of it's contents and yelling, "The mail's here, the mail's here!" Maybe it's true, it doesn't take much to thrill us 'way out here in the countryside.' For that I'm glad.

People of the city, often so entangled in the concrete, plastic and now wireless web often miss the startling simple miracles that make up the patchwork of our lives here in the country.

Take for instance, the moments in late winter when we know that Spring cannot be held back much longer. The day when we spot the first crocus blooms in the receding snow and thrill to the haunting melody of the V-shaped spread of Canadian geese returning north. Our spirit soars with them and winter can no longer restrain it.

I am glad that my family still thrill in the presence of small country miracles for such is The Kingdom of Heaven.

The kitchen door opens and Jared's announcement of our newest spring heifer, freshly born in the south pasture is as awesome to us as ever. We rush out to his Jeep and hurry to check on her. Life embraces us and we feel nourished once again. That salad will sure taste good for supper later!

Spring Has Sprung Salad

    1 pint Asparagus Nubbins (drained)
    8 cups cooked macaroni (drained and chilled)
    1 cup fresh broccoli florets
    1 cup fresh cauliflower florets
    1 bunch radishes (sliced)
    1 bunch green onions (sliced)
    2 cups cooked meat (salmon or chicken)
            Note: Grilled salmon is great in this dish.
1/2 cup fresh parsley
1 small red onion (in rings)
A few leaves of fresh lemon balm (chopped)
Mix all above ingredients well in chilled bowl. Dress with Miracle Whip, your favorite mustard, a little creamy horseradish and 1/2 teaspoon celery seed.

Burnished Splendor

Burnished splendor blankets the autumn days from the ever-changing chill. Morning chores done in jackets precedes shirt-sleeve afternoons. Country pleasures seem to culminate in the heady richness of the early autumn gardens.

Our brussel sprout plants have been defrocked of their foliage, leaving tall thin stalks, covered to the tip with 'little cabbage' as children like to call them. A much maligned vegetable, brussel sprouts, when prepared correctly are one of the aristocrats of the garden patch. Our pickled ones have converted even set-in-stone brussel sprout haters to lovers instead. Try them, you may fall in love again too!

Pickled Brussel Sprouts

Brine:
>2 gallons water
>1 gallon white vinegar (5% acidity)
>2 1/4 cups pickling salt

Spices per jar:
>Pint - 1/4 teaspoon mustard seed
>Quart jar – 1/2 teaspoon mustard seed
>1/2 Gallon jar – 1 teaspoon mustard seed

Approximately 15 pounds raw or frozen brussel sprouts
1 hot red pepper per pint jar
2 hot red peppers per quart jar
4 hot red peppers per 1/2 gallon jar
fresh dill sprigs in each jar

Pack brussel sprouts with spices and fresh dill weed. Place hot peppers in with the sprouts. Pour boiling hot brine into mason jars filled to allow 1/4" headspace. Sprouts must be packed very tightly to avoid floating. Cap and process in boiling water bath the following times:

Pints – 12 minutes
Quarts – 17 minutes
1/2 gallons – 21 minutes
Cool and check seals.

Pickled Brussel Sprouts Uses and Suggestions:
Chilled whole as a relish and appetizer, in salads, snacks and in hot dishes.

Recipe Notes

Rappin' Brussel Sprouts

Bread dough for wrappers:
4-5 cups flour
1 cup whole milk
3 tablespoons sugar
1/2 cup water
1 teaspoon salt
1/4 cup melted butter or margarine
5 teaspoons active dry yeast
Filling:
In skillet brown desired amount of hamburger (about one pound) with 1 chopped onion and 1 tablespoon caraway seed and salt and pepper to taste. Drain fat.

Combine 3 1/2 cups flour, sugar, salt and yeast. Mix well. Heat all liquids together until very warm (120°-130°F). Pour into dry mixture. Mix well. Knead adding additional flour as needed. Dough should be moist, not sticky, and well kneaded. Roll dough out with rolling pin to about 1/4" thick. Cut into squares about size desired. Put one spoon of filling on each square, place one Pickled Brussel Sprout in center and add 1/2 spoon grated mozzarella cheese. Fold up squares to center and pinch. Bake on cookie sheets at 425°F for 12 minutes. Great!

Let this recipe be included in your holiday memories. It can be made as small singles for parties or large for meals.

Scottish Country Wedding

Holidays and country family parties are the perfect excuse for an abundance of rich foods. (As if we needed an excuse!) Each holiday, we look forward to the homecoming of our eldest son Marc and his bride Gretchen. Marc is the only one of our four sons that does not live on Heartland farmland. His career as an attorney has taken him states away from here, but his heart is always here with us.

Marc and Gretchen were married less than a year ago in front of our walk-in fireplace. The wedding was beautiful and the wedding dance in front of the cheerful flames made the snowstorm raging outside seem welcome. Marc's father was so blessed to be able to perform the ceremony, which included some of my family's Scottish heritage.

This old home and our land have been a part of all the births, deaths, marriages and daily trials and triumphs of six generations of my family since my great-grandfather built it. It has stood through the Great Depression, two World Wars, the lunar landing, storms – both small and great, and has never been lived in by anyone other than my family. That's history, that's home!

Marc and Gretchen tell us they "couldn't eat this way very often and still get through doors." We love the festive foods that add to the family times.

LEGACY

Down through eternities time we grow,
From infant to old man – quickly years flow.

Ageless wind blow over land that we claim,
Great-grandfather settled – still the same.

Hints and reminders of heritage survive,
Your love for the land – that same pioneer drive.

Grandmother's faith when she buried her child,
Still anchors her offspring – in a world gone wild.

The feel of the old chair in which they prayed,
Smooth with year's use – their vision stayed.

With tears trickling down, I feel part of that past,
While reading the old family bible – love will last.

Tucked hidden away I find notes on believing,
From Genesis to Revelation – Grandma's faith conceiving.

I'm old yet I'm new, renewing of life,
God's circle of love unbroken - in the midst of strife.

Pickles and Pods

For best results when canning this old fashioned dill pickle, use only fresh, young pickling cucumbers, fresh garlic cloves and hot garden peppers. Dill weed is best homegrown and should be so aromatic that it perfumes your entire kitchen on pickling day. Don't keep your neighbors guessing what type of pickle you're packin'.

So many of our customers remark, "These pickles taste just like the ones my Grandma used to make years ago."

Pickles and Pods Recipe

Makes about 24 pints
Brine:
>2 gallons water
>1 gallon white vinegar (5% acidity)
>2 1/4 cups pickling salt

Spices per jar:
>Pint - 1/4 teaspoon mustard seed
>Quart jar - 1/2 teaspoon mustard seed
>1/2 Qallon jar – 1 teaspoon mustard seed

Wash young pickling cucumbers, red or green jalapenos, garlic cloves and dill weed. In each pint jar use one pepper, 2 sprigs dill weed, three garlic cloves and cucumbers packed tightly to 1/4" headspace. Adjust peppers, garlic, and dill weed accordingly for larger jars.

Bring brine to a boil, pour hot over packed cucumbers. Cap and process in a boiling water bath for 12 minutes for pints, 17 minutes for quarts and 21 minutes for 1/2 gallon jars. Cool and check seals.

Note: Pickles need to set a few weeks before using for best flavor.

Pickles and Pods Uses and Suggestions:
Good with hamburgers, sandwiches, fried potatoes, potato salad and with beans. Also nice on relish trays.

Home Again

We're past the autumn equinox, the dark comes earlier at Heartland now and we once again welcome the change and look forward to long evenings together by the open hearth.

Walking to the old farmhouse, memories fill my thoughts. Loved ones gone before seem somehow present still, for they live on in this realm through my memories of them and their love. They live in the stewardship over this farm and home, until we are together again, should the Lord so bless.

The smell of wood smoke from my new Heartland wood burning cookstove and the glow of golden lamps promise comfort and protection. This simple yet hardy supper prepared from our own homegrown fare and served with cold milk, fresh from Raspberry, my Jersey friend, is one of my favorite country pleasures. It's simple, tasty, wholesome. I'm home once again and my heart is always there. Perhaps that's why it's my Heartland Farm.

A Simple Country Supper

This quick and tasty country supper is one of The Pickle Queen's favorites.

Fried potatoes – country style. Dice up garden potatoes into small cubes or slice. Fry in bacon drippings with chopped onion. Season with your favorite herb mixture, salt and pepper. Serve hot.

Serve fried potatoes with chilled homegrown and home-canned ripe tomatoes. Our home packed Pickles and Pods are the perfect finishing touch. Spicy, crisp and chilled they round out the supper. You'll never miss meat again!

Cherry Picking Time

Our four sons, now grown, still remember the cherry picking and pitting season well. I used to laugh and remind them that "Pitting cherries, one by one, builds character." I still hold to that belief.

Our family pitted many five-gallon bucketfuls of cherries before June gave way to July each year. We were so experienced that we could pit them by hand far faster and better than with the cherry pitter machine – and still retain their shape.

This recipe for Celestial (Pickled) Cherries was created when the buyer for Pier I Imports asked if I could can pickled cherries for them. At the time, I was doing lots of canning for them under their private label, so I gladly agreed. I think you'll be happy I did. They are fabulous – one of our customer favorites.

Celestial Cherries

30 pounds fresh or frozen pitted cherries (pie type)
18 cups sugar
3/4 gallon white vinegar (5% acidity)
2 teaspoons lemon juice
In a spice bag place:
> 1 1/2 cups cinnamon sticks (broken)
> 3/8 cup whole cloves

Tie the bag tightly shut.

Bring syrup to a boil. Add the tightly tied spice bag. Let simmer for 15 minutes. Add the cherries and cook for about 10 minutes. Pack cherries hot into sterile mason jar, pour hot syrup over them, leaving 1/4" headspace. Cap and process in boiling water bath for 7 minutes for pints. Cool and check seals.

Celestial Cherries Uses and Suggestions:

An excellent topping for cheesecake, bagels, grilled and baked meats, fruit salad and stir-fry.

Easter Ham With Celestial Cherries

The unique sweet and sour, spicy cherries with their tangy vinegar add a touch of color and class to the holiday ham. Easy to do for a quick company feast also.

Daffodils and Butterflies

Our little granddaughter, Abby Brooke, loves to hunt for Easter eggs at Heartland. She takes turns with Grandpa and Grammie, before letting each of her three uncles look for them with her. She especially loves for her Aunt Gretchen and Aunt Shan to play with her as she continues the hunt.

What could be sweeter? Easter afternoon, a yard blooming with flowers, the promise of a glorious spring, the smell of newly turned earth and the entire family laughing and playing...for all of us, a time to cherish, a memory of the heart.

Of daffodils and butterflies,
Of trees in sweetest bloom.
Of all thing fair and all things rare,
Of heart's deepest feelings laid bare.
For these I think of you!

From all of us at Heartland, may some of your memories include moments such as these.

BUTTER CHURNS
and DAISIES

There's beauty in simple things, my grandma would say,
In kittens, butter churns and daisies in May.

We've progressed so far, yet sacrificed much,
Simple country pleasures we've lost in the rush.

Dew-laden mornings when summer's just fresh,
Strawberries and cream our pleasure, my we're blessed.

For butter churns, kittens and daisies in May,
I thank God for His goodness in letting me stay!

The Tulip is Only for a Season

Subtle at first, only grey brightens into soft blue of late Winter sky, then the air freshens. Country people resonate; Spring is almost born. We who are part of the land welcome it, and feel our own life renew. Our pulse quickens and spirits soar with cotton-soft days and swelling buds. Soon we will begin to plow pungent earth and drop tiny promises of green Summer into it. The gardener comes to life, forgetting the searing days of August, the weeds of July, and the bugs of June. We need this time to sustain us through harder days.

Spring is one of God's special gifts to His country folks. We who are married to the land, accept it for better or for worse. Each year brings plenty of both. As the Bible tells us, "There is a time for everything, and a season for every activity under heaven." For every life-giving Spring there must also be a killing Winter.

Take time this Spring to enjoy nature's newborn. Fly kites with your children, race the April wind! So often we let life's pressures thwart us from partaking of it's best gifts. The tulip is only for a season.

Recipe Notes

Perky Pineapple

How do you perk up a pineapple? You pickle it! This recipe is awesome.

Syrup:
8 cups sugar
4 cups white vinegar (5% acidity)
Pineapple juice drained from one #10 can of pineapple tidbits
In a spice bag place:
      3/4 cup cinnamon chips or sticks (broken)
      2 teaspoons ground nutmeg
Tie the spice bag tightly.

Bring syrup to a boil, add spice bag and simmer 15 minutes. Cold pack the drained pineapple tidbits into sterile pint jars. Pour the hot syrup over the pineapple and wipe off rim of jar. Cap and process in boiling water bath for 7 minutes for pints. Cool and check seals.

First Grandchild

We always make huge crocks full of sauerkraut every summer. You haven't tasted good kraut until you've tasted homemade. Temperature and weather play key roles in the quality of our finished kraut. Cooler summers make the best kraut.

We were canning our finished sauerkraut the day that Rebecca (our son Trent's wife) went into labor. Our first grandchild was on the way, no time to can kraut! We asked our dear friends Judy and Chris to finish it, which they cheerfully did.

Little Abby is now three and I remember that day every time I open a jar of that 1997 kraut.

Pork and kraut are popular companions. We think you'll enjoy the perk our pineapple adds.

Perky Pineapple Pork

Brown a pork roast in hot oil, searing on all sides. Place into roaster and season with minced garlic, salt and pepper to taste. Add pan drippings to coat bottom of roaster.

On top of stove heat together one pint of un-drained Perky Pineapple with 1 cup light brown sugar. Thicken with 3 tablespoons cornstarch mixed with a small amount of cold water to form a thick paste. Slowly add to pineapple mixture and cook until thickened.

Pour the pineapple glaze over the pork roast. Bake at 350°F for about three hours for a 3-4 pound roast. Time will vary with size of roast and desired degree of doneness.

This dish is good served with our famous home canned sauerkraut. That recipe will be in our next book.

Tough Love

Our style of country living is more that romance – it's often tough love! Picking the young okra pods in the worst heat of a long summer, down hundreds of feet of rows, promotes stamina and is a wonderful character builder.

The yellow blossoms of the tall okra plants are stunning. But that's about all the pleasure you'll receive while picking. Hands and arms get a deposit of sticky, itchy brown okra sap – that if thick enough must be scraped off of hands with a dull knife.

Like many of life's finer rewards, you endure the pain to get the gain - our famous Pickle Cottage Pickled Okra. Our customers say it's the best they have ever tasted.

Pickled Okra

Makes about 6-8 pints
Brine:
> 4 cups water
> 2 cups white or cider vinegar (5% acidity)
> 1/3 cup pickling salt

Spices per jar:
> 1/2 teaspoon dill seed
> 1/8 teaspoon minced garlic
> 2 small red hot chili peppers (*omit for mild Pickled Okra*)

Wash and pack baby okra pods into mason jars with peppers and spices. Bring brine to a boil and fill jars. Cap and process in boiling water bath for 12 minutes. Cool and check seals.

Pickled Okra Uses and Suggestions:
Pickled Okra, traditionally a Southern favorite has expanded its borders. Folks everywhere are discovering the delightful flavor. Best served chilled as a side or on salad platters.

Summer Nights

Our mid-summer night skies are incredible. It's fun to take a salad like this outside and watch the drama. Deepening dusk begins to reveal clusters of light above. We sit mesmerized by the orb rising above the eastern horizon...first pale orange then turning to a perfect pearl as it ascends. Living so close to the land, as we do, we begin to become entangled in its cycles, it's seasons, it's very character. So much so that we can even smell a coming rain or snow and predict the day of the first killing frost. We marvel at the miracle of the creation around us and thank our Creator for allowing us the sheer passion of it's pleasure.

Summertime Supper Salad

Mixed chilled lettuces and spinach leaves torn into bite size pieces
Baby miniature yellow squash (leave whole)
Cherry tomatoes (leave whole)
Diced, chilled cooked ham

Toss together. Then add:
Avocados (arrange in wedges on top)
Sliced Pickled Okra (on top)
Deviled eggs (arrange in halves on top)
Sprinkle ground paprika on top and dress with your favorite dressing.

Recipe Notes

Peck of Pickled Peppers

How many peppers can you pickle? Lots when you use this tasty recipe. Use red, green and yellow sweet bell peppers – ripe with autumn's sweetness and mix them with our spicy brine. You know what they say, "Pickles should be like a woman, beautiful on the outside, good inside and just a little spicy!" This recipe fills the bill.

Brine:
- 2 gallons water
- 1 gallon white vinegar (5% acidity)
- 2 1/4 cups salt

Spices per jar:
- Pint: 1/4 teaspoon mustard seed and three cloves garlic
- Quart: 1/2 teaspoon mustard seed and six cloves garlic
- 1/2 Gallon: 1 teaspoon mustard seed and nine cloves garlic

Wash red, green and yellow bell peppers. Core and cut them into wide strips. Wash fresh dill weed. In each jar place a fresh dill sprig and an even mix of the three peppers leaving a 1/4" headspace. Fill the jars with hot brine. Process pints for 12 minutes, quarts for 17 minutes and 1/2 gallons for 21 minutes in a boiling water bath. Cool and check seals.

Peck of Pickled Peppers Uses and Suggestions:

Good in stir-fry, salads, with beans and all meats. Also good in sandwiches and on hamburgers.

Miss Piggy and Her Piglets

I love to create new stir-fry recipes. Stir-fry is like soup, in that you can mix many different types of mixtures and spices and still achieve excellent results.

This recipe for Perky Peppered Pork uses many of our farm-raised products – Jerusalem artichokes, pork, onions, snow peas and peppers.

Of course our main momma pig, Miss Piggy, doesn't know one of her offspring has made the ultimate sacrifice. We have quite a few momma animals on our farm. The entire family looks forward to our newest baby animal arrivals. They all seem to receive tender, loving care and all receive cute names. I returned home from a recent show to find two new baby piglets – aptly named for their diminutive stature, Pip and Squeak by our daughter Shan.

Perky Peppered Pork

In hot peanut oil in a large wok, stir-fry the following until just done. Leave vegetables tender-crisp.
1-2 pounds sliced pork chop or other tender pork cut.
1/2 pound Shiitake mushrooms (whole)
1/4 pound sliced Jerusalem artichokes
1/2 pint jar Peck of Pickled Peppers (drained)
5 green onions (sliced, include green tops)
1/4 pound snow peas
1 teaspoon chopped fresh ginger root
3 small hot red peppers (sliced)
4 cloves fresh garlic (diced)
2 tablespoons sesame seeds

Add 1/2 cup Pineapple Vinegarette (ours). Add 1/2 to 1 cup soy sauce and about 2 tablespoons Thai seasoning. Heat until bubble. Thicken with a small amount of cornstarch water mixture to gravy-like thickness. Serve over hot rice.

Recipe Notes

Pickled Jalapenos

Favorite food fads change as often as hemlines. Jalapenos are trendy and not exclusive to Tex-Mex cuisine. Their popularity knows no borders. Our Pickled Jalapenos are delicious right out of the jar. With imagination you can create and expand culinary creations using them. They are healthy too! They're loaded with Vitamin C.

Brine:
- 4 cups water
- 2 cups white vinegar (5% acidity)
- 1/3 cup pickling salt

Spices per pint jar:
- 1/2 teaspoon dill seed
- 1/8 teaspoon minced garlic

Heat brine to boiling and simmer. Wash jalapenos. Pack tightly into mason jars with spices. Fill to 1/4" headspace with hot brine. Cap and process in a boiling water bath for 12 minutes for pints. Cool and check seals.

Pickled Jalapenos Uses and Suggestions:

Poppers, salads, Mexican foods, sandwiches, fried potatoes, casseroles, chili and relish platters.

Recipe Notes

Shirley's Sizzling Sandwich

Of course, I'm a little eccentric - all creative people are. That's what I'm often accused of when I make my favorite summertime snack sandwich.

After several sizzling hours at the five acre garden patch, woman-handling my Troybuilt rototiller and the hoe, I love to make this quick sandwich and eat it with a cold glass of my famous iced chocolate mint tea on the side (to help cool the fire). This sandwich is so full of vitamins and natural infection fighters that germs flee at the sound of its name.

"The Triple S"

2 slices white sandwich bread
3-4 thin slices ripe tomatoes
2 slices Pickled Jalapenos
salt to taste

Place the peppers and tomato slices between bread slices, salt lightly.

Simple, tasty, low-cal and healthy. A quick pick-me-upper.

Recipe Notes

Ravishing Red Peppers

This pickle, made from ripe, red hot peppers, is not only good to eat, but is also a conversation piece in your kitchen. The glorious red color and beautiful design create mason jars so pretty you'll hate to open them. Make extras to have some for both décor and eating. You'll agree, they are Ravishing Red Peppers.

Brine:
- 2 gallons water
- 1 gallon white vinegar (5% acidity)
- 2 2/3 cups pickling salt

Spices per jar:
- Pint – 1/4 teaspoon mustard seed and 1/2 teaspoon dill weed
- Quart – 1/2 teaspoon mustard seed and 1 teaspoon dill weed
- 1/2 gallon – 1 teaspoon mustard seed and 2 teaspoons dill weed

Wash red peppers and pack them tightly into jars filled with spices. Add boiling brine leaving 1/4" headspace. Process in a boiling water bath. Pints – 12 minutes; quarts 17 minutes and 1/2 gallons 21 minutes.

Ravishing Red Peppers Uses and Suggestions:

Stuffed with grated cheese and fried, salads, over beans, in soups and casseroles, stir-fry.

Autumn Holdouts

Frost is forecast for the pumpkins. It's time to pick the last of the ripe, red peppers and the remainder of the other autumn holdouts. Walking over the garden, crunching the dried foliage, I experience the annual soul satisfaction that accompanies the completion of our huge garden year.

Growing our own foods is far more than a way to have health, non-polluted foods, or to just be thrifty. It is a deep human instinct, a oneness with the creation we are a part of. The sheer emotional highs and sensory stimulation are reward enough. I gaze into the deep blue that is sky and smell the loam that is soil and know that I have accomplished stewardship over this piece of land. I am leaving it far better than when I first loved it. I have taken and I have given back and the independence that comes from that labor of love satisfies my soul.

Pickled Onions

Onions are one of the hearty, healthy root crops that are so useful, it would be hard to cook without them.

Pickling onions gives them a new taste twist.

Brine:
>12 cups water
>4 cups white vinegar (5% acidity)
>1/2 cup pickling salt

Spices per pint jar:
>1/2 teaspoon dill seed
>1/8 teaspoon minced garlic
>1/8 teaspoon citric acid
>1 hot red pepper (optional)

Wash, peel and wedge onions. Pack tightly into spiced jars with pepper if desired. Cover to 1/4" headspace with boiling brine. Process for 12 minutes in a boiling water bath. Cool and check seals.

Pickled Onions Uses and Suggestions:
Use in salads, soups, casseroles, sandwiches and in beans.

The Note

Food preservation is as old as mankind as we strive to preserve the bounty for the leaner seasons. Root crops such as onions, turnips, carrots, beets and potatoes are easily preserved until spring if properly stored in a root cellar.

I always think of our ancestors and the traditional ways of 'putting up' as I harvest and store autumn's last rewards. Perhaps one memory still stands out to me – I had just moved to our farmhouse and was storing away some of the home-canned foods I had brought with me. I opened the heavy old wooden doors that secure the well-worn pantry storage area. There to my delighted surprise was a handwritten note on the inside of the door, written by a grandmother that died before my birth. She had noted the numbers and types of canned food items she had stored there in 1933. Suddenly, she was not just a picture and stories from my childhood – she was a country woman, flesh of my flesh and now somehow I knew her well. I know she's proud of me; we would have been good friends.

Thank you for the joy of sharing a little of my world with you. I hope that your reality is somehow the better for it. If so, then we have shared ourselves and will carry that always.

Sweet Corn Relish

Most folks love corn! Our Sweet Corn Relish combines the succulent taste of fresh corn with peppers, onions, celery and a feisty mix of spices to create the sweet, spicy combo. Men really go for the flavor. I fact, it's my husband's favorite.

20 pounds corn (cut from the cob)
16 cups chopped celery
3 – 16 oz. Cans pimento pepper
8 cups chopped green bell peppers
15 cups sugar
1 gallon white or cider vinegar (5% acidity)
4 cups chopped onion
1/2 cup salt
1/4 cup allspice
1/4 cup turmeric
1/2 cup dry mustard
1 cup + 1 tablespoon flour mixed with 2 cups water – mix to paste

Mix the vegetables, spices, sugar and vinegar. Heat to simmer 15 minutes. Add the flour and water paste quickly and stir in well to avoid lumps. Simmer 10 minutes more or until just bubbly. Pack hot into sterile mason jars. Wipe rim of jar and cap. Process pints for 7 minutes in a boiling water bath. Cool and check seals.

Sweet Corn Relish Uses and Suggestions:

Sweet Corn Relish can be 'relished' in sandwiches, beans, casseroles, omelets, cornbread and salads.

Fruit of the Womb

We who truly still do live off the land appreciate hearty simple fare when we come in to eat, especially during the hectic pace of early spring plowing and planting, or in the stressful yet fun calving season when we often serve as midwives to our growing herd of cows (which at Heartland are also our friends).

At Heartland Farm, we have spent years breeding and building a herd of old-fashioned breeds of dairy cows for our family use. We enjoy fresh raw milk, butter, ice cream and all types of homemade cheeses.

It's amazing how smart and loving a dairy cow and calf can be when they receive lots of attention like ours do.

For fun, we started naming our dairy cows after types of fruits and we jokingly call the little red dairy barn, "the fruit of the womb."

At present, Raspberry, Applesauce, Mulberry, Peaches, Cherry, Plum and Sugarplum are at home in the clover grass pastures of Heartland. Raspberry, our little fawn-colored Jersey is my favorite and she returns my favor.

This casserole can be prepared ahead to refrigerate or freeze back for your busy seasons. The addition of Sweet Corn Relish to the cornbread topping adds moistness and zest to this hearty main dish.

Cowboy Casserole

In a 9" by 13" baking dish, fill the bottom half full of you favorite chili. On top of the chili, place large spoonfuls of the cornbread recipe below. Spread the cornbread batter evenly over the chili. You can add sliced Pickled Jalapenos over the top for additional heat if desired.

Cornbread Topping:
1 1/2 cups yellow cornmeal
1/2 cup flour
4 teaspoon baking powder
1/2 teaspoon salt
1 cup milk
1/4 cup cooking oil
1 beaten egg

Mix dry ingredients evenly. Add milk, egg, and oil to the dry mixture. Stir only enough to moisten. Put evenly on top of chili and bake at 425°F for 25 minutes.

Recipe Notes

Corny Pasta Salad

Cool, refreshing, yet hearty. Good for a main or side dish.
1 pint Corn Relish
2 quarts cooked, cooled and drained pasta of your choice
1/2 cup chopped green pepper
1/4 cup chopped red onion
Miracle Whip or mayonnaise to taste
Mustard to taste
1/2 teaspoon celery seed

Mix all ingredients well. Dress with Miracle Whip or mayonnaise and mustard until creamy. Sprinkle paprika on top. Garnish with fresh parsley sprigs.

The Corn Belt Special

1 bar softened cream cheese
1/2 pint Sweet Corn Relish

Mix well until spread-able and creamy. Makes a good dip for snack nights or for parties.

Recipe Notes

Calico Beans

Remember the three-bean salad your mom made you eat? This is our peppy, pickled version. Great as a side or in combination with both hot and cold recipes. Fun to fix and delightful to serve.

1 - #10 can kidney beans
1 - #10 can wax beans
1 - #10 can green beans
Mix together in a large bowl
Brine:
>5 cups water
>5 cups white vinegar (5% acidity)
>3/8 cup pickling salt

Spices per pint jar:
>1/2 teaspoon mustard seed
>1/2 teaspoon dill seed
>1/4 teaspoon minced garlic
>1/4 teaspoon hot red pepper flakes

Spice jars. Pack bean mixture into sterile mason jars. Fill with boiling brine leaving 1/4" headspace. Cap and process in boiling water bath for 12 minutes. Cool and check seals.

Calico Beans Uses and Suggestions:

Calico Beans are great in chili, salads, Tex-Mex dishes, soups and casseroles. They can be served alone as a side.

Memories of the Heart

Most cherished family memories are not always the big events of life, but often the mundane moments when times seems to pause for a heartbeat and frame the picture which we will never forget and mark the moments that become eternal. These are the memories that cause the old to reflect and smile once again and the young to forge new memories in the mold of the past.

Sometimes it's as simple as picking up pebbles on a walk together or cuddling by the fire for one last cup of tea before bed.

One such memory in our family is our yearly trip to cut the family Christmas tree, usually reserved for the day following Thanksgiving. We all pile into the big truck and head north to explore for the 'best one yet' – which some years is simply the 'biggest one yet.' As the boys, now all grown, devise creative new ways to bring it into the main room and keep it standing upright.

Hot soup is the favorite choice for supper. We begin to unwrap and discuss each treasured childhood memory before hanging them once more on our tree. Calico Chili warms both body and spirit on just such an occasion.

Calico Chili

Makes a big pot
2 pounds ground hamburger
1 pound ground pork sausage
1 large onion chopped
Brown and drain off fat
Add:
3 quarts home-canned tomatoes – cut up a little
2 tablespoons chopped oregano – fresh or dried
salt to taste
ground cumin to taste
ground dark chili powder to taste (I use lots!)
1 1/2 tablespoons minced garlic
1 quart cooked and drained pinto beans (can be canned)
1 quart cooked and drained kidney beans (can be canned)
1 pint drained Calico Beans

Mix all in large heavy pot, cook slowly until bubbly, thick and tasty. Remember your spices will taste stronger as the chili cooks down. Every family likes the chili spiced a little differently. Taste as you go, to suit your family taste. We like it spicy!

This dish freezes and cans very well.

Recipe Notes

Calico Taco Salad

Makes one large bowl
1 head iceberg lettuce (chopped)
1 head buttercrunch lettuce (chopped)
1 large can kidney beans (drained)
1 large can black olives (drained and sliced)
6 – 10 sliced Pickled Jalapenos (adjust to taste)
6 – 12 Roma tomatoes (chopped)
1/4 to 1/2 cup cilantro leaves (adjust to taste)
1 jar Calico Beans (drained)
1 very large bag taco chips (break coarsely)
2 cups grated cheddar cheese

Brown together and drain off fat:
2 pounds hamburger
chili seasoning to taste
cumin to taste
salt and pepper to taste
1/2 teaspoon minced garlic

Cool hamburger mixture then add to lettuce mixture. Dress with salsa or dressing of your choice.

Southern Heritage

Heritage reminds us in diverse ways of our ancestors and their preferences. I've often been accused of 'cookin' in that famous Southern style, yet living north of the Mason-Dixon line seems to contradict that observation. Not really, you see my roots are in the south on my mother's side. They were originally one of the nine families that founded the area later to become The Smokey Mountain National Park in North Carolina. Perhaps that explains my passion for fried green tomatoes and my tendency to say, "ya'll" too much.

Dilly Southwest Green Tomatoes are an original recipe created by the Pickle Queen herself following in the taste tradition of fried green tomatoes.

For the ultimate taste, the green tomatoes you use for these pickles, must be very fresh, very green and packed with plenty of freshly cut dill weed. Good eatin' to ya'll!

Dilly Green Southwest Tomatoes

Brine:
- 2 gallons water
- 1 gallon white vinegar (5% acidity)
- 2 1/4 cups pickling salt

Spices per jar:
- Pint - 1/4 teaspoon mustard seed and 1 hot pepper
- Quart - 1/2 teaspoon mustard seed and 2 hot peppers
- 1/2 gallon - 1 teaspoon mustard seed and 4 hot peppers

Wash and slice green tomatoes. Pack into spiced jars using fresh dill weed. Add peppers to accent the look. Place several cloves of fresh garlic into each jar. Pour boiling brine into packed jars, leaving 1/4" headspace. Process in a boiling water bath as follows: pints – 12 minutes; quarts – 17 minutes; 1/2 gallon – 21 minutes. Cool and check seals.

Dilly Green Southwest Tomatoes Uses and Suggestions:
These green tomatoes *make* a grilled hamburger, are fabulous in vegetable salads, good with ham and beans and even make a lowly bologna sandwich palatable.

Recipe Notes

Grilled Southwest Salad

1 pound grilled hamburger patties (break in pieces)
3 pounds mixed greens: red and green lettuce, spinach leaves, Romaine lettuce
A few fresh cilantro sprigs
A few fresh dill sprigs
6 sliced Pickled Jalapenos
1 pint Southwest Dilly Green Tomatoes (drained)
1 pint cherry tomatoes
2 red sweet bell peppers
1/2 cup black olives

Mix together well. Dress with an oil and vinegar dressing. (It can be mixed with the reserved liquid from the Southwest Dilly Green Tomatoes). Sprinkle a mixture of yellow and white grated cheeses on top and spicy toasted croutons.

Recipe Notes

Honey – D – Green Tomatoes

When the hit movie, "Fried Green Tomatoes" came out, my first customer, Bloomingdale's buyer Alan Palmer, called me and asked me to create a green tomato pickle to honor the occasion. I did! I love them, he loved them and it seems all of you love them too!

With a flavor similar to Chow-Chow, our Honey – D – Green Tomatoes are a hit matched with catfish. The richness of natural honey combines with an array of spices to accent the taste of summer in the country has made them one of our most requested items.

16 cups sugar
12 cups white vinegar (5% acidity)
2 1/4 cups pure, natural honey
2 tablespoons dry mustard
2 tablespoons whole cloves
2 tablespoons cinnamon chips
2 tablespoons powdered ginger
1 tablespoons celery seed

Bring to a simmer and add:
8 cups sliced green peppers
5 cups sliced onions
20 oz. Diced red pimento pepper
14 cups sliced green tomatoes

Bring back to a bubbly simmer and pack hot into mason jars. Wipe off rim of jars well and cap. Process pints for 7 minutes in a boiling water bath. Cool and check seals.

Honey – D – Green Tomatoes Uses and Suggestions:
This recipe is truly multi-purpose…great baked over a variety of meats, served with fried fish, over baked beans and right out of the jar.

Recipe Notes

Dinner Bell

Where is lunch really dinner and dinner is actually supper? At Heartland Farm we still follow the old farm tradition of our largest meal at noon – dinner and our smallest in the evening – supper.

I soon learned to make myself clear which time of the day dinner is when we invite our city friends for a meal. When the dinner bell rings (yes, we have one) or mom hollers out the kitchen door, "Dinner's ready," the family knows it's mid-day and time for the daily feast of farm fare.

I like recipes like this one that can be cooking slowly all morning while I'm in our five-acre garden, or splitting wood or in my upstairs office writing by the fireplace. Add a salad and some crunchy bread to balance out this meal.

Honeyed Swiss Chicken

This recipe can be baked in the oven or overnight/all day in your crock pot. Easy and good enough to impress company.

Place chicken breasts in shallow baking casserole or in a crock pot. Lightly salt and sprinkle garlic on breasts. Cover breasts with Honey – D – Green Tomatoes and liquid. Cover well and bake at 300°F for two hours or crock pot on low for 10-12 hours depending on size of chicken breasts.

Recipe Notes

Pickled Garlic

Garlic! Garlic! Garlic! With all of the garlic we've sold, I think every vampire in America was worried. Without a doubt, our best seller, Pickled Garlic brings rave reviews. Hearty and healthy, our Pickled Garlic will be the hit of your home too. Besides the taste, our customers tell us their health is better while eating our garlic.

Brine:
>2 gallons water
>1 gallon white vinegar (5% acidity)
>2 1/4 cups pickling salt

Spices per jar:
>Pint - 1/2 teaspoon mustard seed, 1 jalapeno and 1 sprig of dill weed
>
>Quart - 1/2 teaspoon mustard seed, 2 jalapenos and 2 sprigs of dill weed
>
>° Gallon - 1 teaspoon mustard seed, 4 jalapenos and 4 sprigs dill weed

Pack raw, peeled garlic into jars with spices dill weed and jalapenos – red or green. Leave 1/2" headspace. Fill jars with boiling brine to 1/4" headspace. Cap and process in boiling water bath as follows: pints – 12 minutes; quarts – 17 minutes; 1/2 gallons – 21 minutes. Cool and check seals.

Pickled Garlic Uses and Suggestions:
Pickle Cottage Pickled Garlic is so good as a snack, in salads, mashed potatoes, casseroles, stir-fry, sautéed in butter, with grilled meats and diced in a bowl of beans. The brine from our garlic combines with olive oil to make a good dressing also.

Recipe Notes

Ritzy Garlic

1 box Ritz snack crackers
1 8 oz. Box softened cream cheese (can also use homemade)
1 pint Pickled Garlic

Spread softened cream cheese on each cracker, top with a clove of Pickled Garlic. Serve it and you'll be asked to bring it to every party after that!

Garlic Taters

To a large pot of peeled Irish potatoes in water, add Pickled Garlic cloves to taste – about 12. Cook with potatoes until potatoes are done. Drain and mash the garlic with the potatoes. Salt to taste. Add sour cream and whip to proper consistency for mashed potatoes. Serve with a pat of butter in the middle of bowl.

Recipe Notes

Bread and Butter Pickles

Perhaps no other pickle brings back American memories of Thanksgiving dinner at Grandma's house or mom in the kitchen in late summer preserving the garden bounty, quite as much as Bread and Butter Pickles.

A classic founded in our German heritage of 'seven sweets and seven sours,' this beloved old favorite is offered here in its original, traditional recipe, which dates back to pioneer times. Don't be fooled by modern versions commercially sold as Bread and Butters. Not all pickles are created equal! Bread and Butter Pickles are to pickles what apple pie is to pie!

Syrup:
3 cups cider vinegar or white (5% acidity)
3 cups sugar
1 tablespoon salt
1 teaspoon mustard seed
1 teaspoon celery seed
1 teaspoon turmeric
Heat syrup until boiling, stirring well. Add the following:
15 cucumbers (sliced thin) leave peels on
3 onions (sliced and broken into rings)
Cook until almost bubbly – about 10 – 15 minutes. After cooked to proper doneness, pack hot into mason jars. Fill with hot syrup leaving 1/4" headspace. Wipe rim of jars and cap. Process pints in boiling water bath for 7 minutes. Cool and check seals.

Bread and Butter Pickles Uses and Suggestions:
Bread and Butters are good on all sandwiches and as a snack. Traditional for relish trays.

Recipe Notes

The Monday Night Special

Sunday dinner with the entire family around the table featured roast beef, done to perfection. As with many of us, you appreciate those leftovers on Monday night after the classic, "It's Monday, what can I say?" day has passed.

Here's a great sandwich recipe featuring left-over roast beef and homemade Bread and Butter Pickles. Even Mondays can be fun days!

On whole-wheat bread, either toasted or grilled, spread creamy horseradish sauce (homemade is best). Add slices of Bread and Butter Pickles, lettuce, thinly sliced tomatoes, dark stone-ground mustard and generous slabs of chilled roast beef. Very good served with hot potato soup or cream of broccoli soup.

Recipe Notes

Racy Raspberries

Our customers tell us that raspberries are among their favorite fruits. This racy, pickled recipe for raspberries has even been served to heads of state and for several parties given for the stars.

Syrup:
6 cups sugar
2 cups white vinegar (5% acidity)
4 quarts raspberries (frozen or fresh)
Spice bag:
3 tablespoons cinnamon chips
1/2 teaspoon ground nutmeg

Bring syrup with spice bag tied and in the syrup to a boil. Boil gently for 5 minutes. Add raspberries, cook gently for 1 more minute. Pack hot into jars. Process 7 minutes for pints in a boiling water bath. Cool and check seals.

Racy Raspberries Uses and Suggestions:
Toppings for cheesecake, desserts, bagels, all meats, and mixed in glazes and sauces.

Kansas Buttermilk Pie
with Racy Raspberries

I was asked by the state of Kansas to create a special recipe that would combine one of our pickles with an old-fashioned Kansas pioneer recipe. This was to represent the state of Kansas at the Earl's Court in London, England, where the Queen of England would be present.

This recipe was honored in England. It is truly something old and something new!

Our hope, as we have shared both our foods and our hearts with you, is just that, the merging of the best of both the past and the present, to enrich the future.

Kansas Buttermilk Pie with Racy Raspberries

I always use our homemade buttermilk, but you can also use commercial buttermilk and get excellent results.

- 1 – 9" pie crust, baked and cooled
- 6 tablespoons softened butter
- 1 1/2 cups sugar
- 2 eggs, separated
- 3 tablespoons flour
- 1 1/2 cups buttermilk
- 2 teaspoons lemon juice
- 1/4 teaspoon ground cloves
- 1 teaspoon ground cinnamon
- 1/2 teaspoon nutmeg

Cream butter and sugar until light. Add egg yolks, one at a time, beating after each addition. Combine flour and spices and beat into the butter mixture. Still beating, pour in the buttermilk in a thin stream. Stir in lemon juice. Whip the egg whites until they stand in peaks. Gently fold them into the buttermilk batter. Pour into pie crust and bake at 350°F until pie is firm – about 40 minutes. Chill. After chilled, top with chilled Racy Raspberries and serve.

Recipe Notes

Blueberry Bash

Pickled Blueberries are such a happy surprise. While retaining their sweetness, the pickling perks up the taste.

Syrup:
2 cups white vinegar (5% acidity)
6 cups sugar
Spice bag:
3 tablespoons cinnamon chips
1/2 teaspoon ground nutmeg
4 quarts fresh or frozen blueberries

Tie spices in cloth bag. Bring spices and syrup to a boil. Boil gently for 5 minutes. Add blueberries and cook for one minute. Pack hot. Cover with hot syrup. Wipe rims of jars and seal. Process pints 7 minutes in boiling water bath. Cool and check seals.

Blueberry Bash Uses and Suggestions:
Toppings for desserts, cheesecake, meats, good in pancakes and can be used in breads.

A Heartland Christmas

Our family always celebrates Christmas Eve with a large traditional feast. This year will be a roast goose from our flock. After the meal, we sit by the fire and open our gifts as we share in the joy of celebrating our Lord's birth.

On Christmas morning, we enjoy a mid-morning brunch. Dad always makes the best pancakes. The addition of our Pickled Blueberries is a hit.

Like most good cooks, Barry and I don't measure too often. We just taste and dump. For your benefit, he will measure to be sure they will turn out right for your Christmas brunch.

Keeping this thought, I remember my Grandma Renner's best ever bread recipe. It began … Take a large wooden bowl, fill halfway with flour. If you didn't have Granny's bowl, you were out of luck! She was still one of the best cooks the Lord ever created.

Dad's Christmas Brunch Pancakes

1 cup white flour
1 cup whole wheat flour
1/2 cup yellow corn meal
1 teaspoon salt
2 tablespoon baking powder
3 tablespoons sugar
Mix all dry ingredients together well.
Add:
1 egg
1/4 cup vegetable oil
1 cup whole milk (minimum) Use more until desired batter consistency is achieved. For heartier pancakes, leave batter thicker. For softer pancakes, leave batter thinner.

Add 1/2 pint drained Blueberry Bash to batter, gently fold in the fruit. Liquid from the Blueberry Bash can be used in the syrup or is good in hot tea.

Very lightly grease your griddle. Pour 1/3 to 1/2 cup batter for each pancake onto hot griddle. Flip pancakes when air bubbles in pancakes begin to break open and stay open. Cook until evenly brown on both sides.

Enjoy and Merry Christmas!

The Christmas Gift

"God works in mysterious ways," it is said. Let me tell you about the special Christmas gift I received one Christmas morning – the gift that has changed my life in unexpected ways. The gift that came from a simple heart prayer.

For years, I'd longed to have a house cat – a special furry feline friend. I'd sometimes imagine what he'd be like: long-haired, white feet and face, pink nose, smart (hopefully not smarter than me), eccentric, funny and loyal and loving to a fault.

I was resigned to the real possibility that my feline fantasy would remain just that, only a hope, an unspoken prayer. My husband, who is so loving and always tries to fulfill my every desire, was adamant, "NO HOUSE CAT! God made cats to live outdoors and catch mice. I like cats, just not in the house!" he informed me more than once.

The subject seemed closed, yet I never quit thinking how special it would be to have the 'puddy' of my dreams. I would even say little prayers from time to time, "Lord, I sure would love…if it's your will."

Years passed. Farm cats came and farm cats went. A farm cat's life is quickly spent considering all the pitfalls such as coyotes, weather, stray dogs, cattle's hooves and the list goes on.

Sometimes I'd fall in love with a farm cat and be reminded once more, "Don't get any ideas. We are not going to have a house cat." So the cycle of birth and death continued, as spring usually blessed us with several new litters of fluff-balls and winter often took them away.

Then it happened. A series of events that only God could arrange, a series of events that eventually answered my prayer.

That Christmas morning began in sweet serenity as the family gathered for the traditional Christmas morning brunch. Afterwards, Jared, our youngest son, came back from the barn loft with unusual news…winter births of kittens are not common on farms and we had never heard of kittens being born on Christmas morning! Jared announced, "Hey guys, you should come see the new litter of baby kittens that were just born in the hay loft. They're really cute!"

The entire litter was adorable, yet one by one, they met up with accidents, until only one of the six remained. He was so pretty – white feet, face and tummy, long-haired, loving, smart, pink nose. I couldn't help myself – it was love at first cuddle. He was officially christened Sparky, but soon adopted the nickname, Spiggs, and so Spiggs it is.

Spiggs began his life the normal Heartland way – outdoors. He loved to romp with the other animals but he and I were special friends right from the start. We were bonding.

Then it happened. We returned home from a prolonged business trip to find him hurt and possibly dying in a few days. Spiggs had been run over and left for dead, his left front leg totally crushed and his tail broken. He must have suffered for several days before we returned as gangrene had set it and he was gravely ill. He was so sick that he couldn't move from his hiding spot. That is until he heard my voice calling him. He mustered up strength enough to come to me and collapsed at my feet – looking horrible and smelling worse!

"Barry, please let me take him to the vet. I know it's expensive. I'll make up the extra myself," I pleaded. "You can't just let him lay here and die!" Remember, on a working farm, death is not a stranger. We live very close to hard realities.

I don't know if it was my pain or Spiggs', but Barry's heart softened. "Ok, call the vet. You can carry him and I'll drive." The vet was surprised Spiggs was still alive, he was so sick. I just kept holding him and telling him I loved him and needed him and praying for him to recover.

Recover he did. Spiggs now had only three legs and a little crook on the end of his fluffy tail. But he was mine once more.

The vet reminded us that he would not be able to survive outdoors in the country, with only three legs so if we hoped to keep him alive, a house cat he must be. My dear husband could not betray his kind heart. "You can make him your house cat. I'm not going to turn him out to a certain death," Barry said with resigned resolve.

Spiggs is now a member of our family, much beloved by all of us. Yet, he's still my cat, as I am his person. He daily teaches us lessons in loyalty, compassion, comfort, humor and gentleness. God picked him out for me and sent him to me on Christmas morning in a humble little barn.

Through a divine plan, I have come to experience once more, God's special gift of love over my life – in even small details, through His Christmas gift to me.

Recipe Notes

Olives & Eve

Our hangtag reads, "Finally a product so tempting, you'll feel like Adam in the Garden of Eden." Huge imported Spanish Queen olives pickled in our now, not so secret recipe, can by your new favorite party snack too.

As the Pickle Queen, I always loved coming up with the catchy names for the new pickles that I had just given birth to. Olives & Eve always evokes a question and a smile. Serve your Adam some of this tempting fruit!

Brine:
    3 gallons water
    1 gallon white vinegar (5% acidity)
    1 cup pickling salt

Spices per jar:
    Pint – 1/2 teaspoon dill seed, 1/4 teaspoon garlic and 1 hot pepper
    Quart – 1 teaspoon dill seed, 1/2 teaspoon garlic and 2 hot peppers
    1/2 gallon – 2 teaspoons dill seed, 1 teaspoon garlic, and 4 hot peppers

Onion wedges – use 1/6 as much as olives

Spice jars. Pack Spanish Queen olives into spiced jars with onions and peppers. Bring brine to a boil. Pour over tightly packed olives and onions to leave 1/4" headspace. Cap and process in a boiling water bath as follows:

Pints – 12 minutes; quarts – 17 minutes; 1/2 gallon – 21 minutes. Remove, cool and check seals.

Olives & Eve Uses and Suggestions:
    Use in salads, drinks, snacks, sandwiches, casseroles, soups and party trays.

Gathering the Eggs

Gathering the evening eggs from our chickens and putting the ducks and geese into the pens for the night is always fun. Our collection of feathered friends has expanded this year from chickens and turkeys to include ducks and geese also. From Mabel – our favorite turkey who likes to tour the farmyards and makes sure all creatures (including the two-legged ones) were meeting with her approved way of doing things – to the cute pranks of the ducks and geese. The poultry always evoke comments form our visitors. You might be amazed at the perceptiveness of the barnyard members of our country family, if given enough love and attention.

With chicken from our flocks, homemade cheese from our cows and vegetables from our gardens, we don't need to shop at a grocery store. Our grocery store is our farm. But it is fun to purchase a few foods that we can't grow, such as olives. Eve's Scalloped Chicken combines the best of both worlds.

Eve's Scalloped Chicken

    1 large hen – cooked in boiling water until tender (about 2 1/2 to 3 1/2 hours) in a large pot. Remove meat from bones and reserve broth for cooking.
    1 cup chopped onion
    1 1/2 cups Velveeta cheese (diced) or homemade
    1/2 teaspoon black pepper
    1/2 teaspoon salt
    2 eggs – beaten
    1 can cream of mushroom soup
    2 large boxes Ritz crackers
    1 pint Olives & Eve (drained and sliced)

    Break 1 1/2 boxes crackers up coarsely. Mix together well all other ingredients. Spread evenly into large, somewhat flat casserole dish. Top with other 1/2 box of Ritz crackers, broken coarsely. Sprinkle top with paprika. Option: More Olives & Eve can be used on top if desired.
    Bake 325°F for 1 hour.

Recipe Notes

Sweet Pickle Relish

Both Barry and I have strong pioneer bloodlines, which accounts in part for our firm love of the land and our 'in-your-face' independent, patriotic natures.

Our recipe for Sweet Pickle Relish was carried to Kansas on a wagon train in the early 1900's and has been in our family since.

I couldn't make my potato salad or meat salad sandwiches taste right without it. Store-bought just isn't the same.

Makes 4 pints
8 cups ground cucumbers
2 cups ground onion
1/4 cup pickling salt
3 cups sugar
1 1/2 cups cider vinegar
1 teaspoon turmeric
1 stick cinnamon
1 teaspoon celery seed
1 teaspoon ground allspice

Combine cucumbers, onions and salt. Let stand 20 minutes. Drain well. Combine remaining ingredients with drained cucumber mixture and simmer for 20 minutes. Remove cinnamon stick. Pack hot relish into jars. Seal and process pints for 7 minutes in boiling water bath. Cool and check seals.

Sweet Pickle Relish Uses and Suggestions:
Add to potato, pasta and meat salads. Use for sandwiches and with beans.

Recipe Notes

Garden Potato Salad

Some foods are always in style and good taste. Potato salad stands the test of timeless taste. Our country version features a chunky mix of garden grown potatoes, green onions, farm-fresh eggs and of course our Sweet Pickle Relish.

3 pounds potatoes, cooked, diced and drained
6 hard-boiled eggs, peeled and diced
6 green onions, chopped
1 tablespoon celery seed
salt to taste
Miracle Whip and mustard to taste
1/2 pint Sweet Pickle Relish

Mix all ingredients until creamy. Chill and enjoy. Simple but super.

Recipe Notes

A Traditional Thanksgiving

At Heartland, we hold to country tradition concerning Thanksgiving. It is not 'turkey day' or 'TV day' or a day for the women to shop while the men watch football.

Instead, while our feast is cooking, the family gathers to give thanks in the morning, before we enjoy our favorite Thanksgiving dishes with our homegrown turkey. Each member of the family in turn tells what he or she has been most thankful for in the past year. We reflect, share and thank God for His blessings upon us and our land.

I'll never forget the Thanksgiving that our homegrown and butchered Tom turkey was too big to fit in any of our roasters. In a panic, we got the biggest commercial pot that would still fit into our largest oven, and made Tom a final resting place. It took two of us to carry him to the oven. That gave new meaning to leftovers! Try this recipe to spice up some of your holiday leftovers.

Turkey Salad Sandwiches

Grind leftover turkey. Mix with chopped hard-boiled eggs, Sweet Pickle Relish, Miracle Whip, mustard and chopped red bell peppers. Mix well and chill.

Whole wheat or rye breads are good with Turkey Salad. It's also nice served on lettuce leaves for a light, low-calorie lunch.

Pickled Asparagus

Asparagus is spring – spring is asparagus! To me, it truly is the fabled food of the gods. I love its delicate, green, sophisticated flavor. At its peak of perfection, picked fresh and rushed to our cannery to be pickled in our special brine, Pickled Asparagus should be served at springtime meals or anytime you want to experience April in August.

Brine:
    16 cups water
    4 cups white vinegar (5% acidity)
    3/4 cup pickling salt
    1/32 teaspoon tartaric acid (optional – helps keep asparagus fresher)

Spices per pint jar:
    1/2 teaspoon pickling spice
    1/2 teaspoon dill seed
    1/8 teaspoon minced garlic

Put spices in jars. Cut tender asparagus tips in lengths to fit length of mason jars, allowing 1/4" headspace. Pack the asparagus in jars, tips up. Bring brine to boil and fill jars to within 1/4" of top. Process in boiling water bath for 12 minutes. Cool and check seals.

Pickled Asparagus Uses and Suggestions:
This pickle is so gourmet, it is truly multi-faceted. Great as a side, in salads, and in gourmet dishes.

The Smell of Wood Smoke

The art, (for it is an art) of outdoor cookery is an ancient one. Each type of wood gives its unique character to the food grilled over it. Experiment when smoking and grilling outdoors – you may be surprised to discover some woods you love to use are not the ones you would have thought of at first. For instance, the common and little regarded Siberian Elm wood imparts a wonderful smoky zest to foods so fortunate to be grilled over it. Use your favorite wood and enjoy our Asparagus Pork Roll-ups at your next cookout!

Asparagus Pork Roll-ups with Herb Butter
Thinly slice a nice cut of pork roast or pork tenderloin. Marinate pork in Pickled Asparagus brine drained from Picked Asparagus, for at least 6 hours in refrigerator.
Place one stalk of Pickled Asparagus in the middle of each pork slice. Also place two strips of fresh red sweet bell pepper with the asparagus. Roll up the pork around the vegetables and secure with skewers. Grill until just done. Serve hot with hot herb butter drizzled over it.

Hot Herb Butter
Melt 1 cup butter with 1 teaspoon garlic (chopped or minced), 2 teaspoons fresh thyme and 1 teaspoon sweet marjoram. Mix well and serve.

Recipe Notes

Sweet Summer Medley

The blossom that is spring turns, as it should, to the fruit that is summer. Now is the time to can some of its blessings. Combining yellow and green summer squash, with bell peppers, onions and our Bread and Butter style syrup creates a medley of taste. Just think of it this way – you won't have to lock your doors and hide from the neighbors during zucchini season!

Syrup:
4 cups sugar
3 cups white vinegar (5% acidity)
1 tablespoon celery seed
1 teaspoon turmeric
Vegetables:
2 cups sliced green bell peppers
8 cups yellow summer squash, sliced
8 cups green summer squash, sliced
4 cups sliced onion
6 oz. Diced red pimento pepper

Bring syrup to a boil. Add the vegetables and cook slowly for 15 to 20 minutes. Pack hot into sterile mason jars. Pour hot syrup over it to 1/4" headspace. Wipe rims of jars. Process pints 7 minutes in boiling water bath. Cool and check seals.

Sweet Summer Medley Uses and Suggestions:
Use on sandwiches, in salads and it's good as a side.
Pork Cutlet Sandwiches
Dip pork cutlets in a mixture of 2 well-beaten eggs and 1 cup cream. Bread them in a mixture of: 1/2 cup yellow corn meal, 1/2 cup flour, 1 teaspoon minced garlic, 1/4 teaspoon red pepper flakes, 1 teaspoon salt, 1/2 teaspoon black pepper. Fry breaded pork cutlets in hot oil. Drain well.

To make sandwiches, spread creamy horseradish sauce onto sesame-seed buns. Place a liberal layer of Sweet Summer Medley chips onto buns. Place fried pork cutlets on buns accented with lettuce leaves. This is good with salad in summer and soup in winter.

Food is An Art

I'm often amazed and shocked by the sheer disdain that many women hold for the art (yes, art!) of cooking today. Food is more than life-giving. It's fun, it's creative, it's comforting, it's stimulating, it's another form of art!

Perhaps it can be blamed in part on a society that holds little regard for domestic skills unless they are highly marketable as mine are. If you are among those who swear they will never cook or can, please reconsider. You are missing out on one of life's basic joys. This very simple recipe is a good one to start with, it's easy and quick.

Pickled Carrots

Brine:
- 12 cups water
- 4 cups white vinegar (5% acidity)
- 3/4 cup pickling salt

Spices per pint jar:
- 1/2 teaspoon pickling spice
- 1/2 teaspoon dill seed
- 1/8 teaspoon minced garlic
- 1 hot pepper (optional)

Pack baby or young carrot sticks into pre-spiced mason jars. Pour boiling brine over carrots. Cap and process pints in boiling water bath for 12 minutes. Cool and check seals.

Pickled Carrots Uses and Suggestions:
Relish trays, snacks and salads.

Pickled Carrot Pinwheels
On a pretty party tray, arrange the following in pinwheels: Pickled Carrots, strips of cold cuts, strips of yellow and white chesses, peeled cold shrimp, green pepper strips and red sweet pepper strips. Serve with your favorite vegetable dip or Ranch dressing.

Recipe Notes

Sweet Red Relish

Are you a Pickled Beet lover? If so, this relish will be a favorite for you. To relish this relish made from chopped beets, use as you would other relishes for a colorful and different flare.

Syrup:
3 cups cider vinegar
4 cups sugar
2 teaspoon salt
1/2 teaspoon ground cloves
1/2 teaspoon cinnamon
Spice bag:
2 tablespoons pickling spice
6 oz. Diced red pimento pepper
2 cups diced beets (cooked and peeled)
1/2 cup diced onions (peeled)

Bring syrup to a boil. Add the prepared vegetables and simmer for 15 minutes. Pack hot into mason jars, leaving 1/4" headspace. Wipe rims of jars. Process in a boiling water bath for 7 minutes for pints. Cool and check seals.

Tuesday's Tuna Teasers

To combat a boring Tuesday lunch of 'tuna again?' try this twist.

1 hard-boiled egg (peeled and chopped)
1 can tuna
1/2 cup Sweet Red Relish
Miracle Whip (enough to make it creamy)

Serve on white sandwich bread.

Recipe Notes

Marvelous Mandarin Oranges

This is the Pickle Queen's favorite pickled fruit. I eat them right out of the jar – without sharing! Excellent in cooking also.

Syrup:
8 cups sugar
4 cups white vinegar (5% acidity)
Juice from 1 - #10 can mandarin oranges
Spice bag:
3/4 cup cinnamon chips
2 teaspoons ground nutmeg

Bring syrup to a boil with spice bag. Put the #10 can of oranges into the syrup. Heat for a few minutes. Pack hot into pint jars and fill with hot syrup. Wipe rims and cap. Process in boiling water bath for 7 minutes. Cool and check seals.

Marvelous Mandarin Oranges Uses and Suggestions:
Use in stir-fries, on desserts, in fruit salads and with meats.

Recipe Notes

Orange and Chicken Stir-fry

Don't be afraid to vary stir-fry ingredients. I often change them according to what's in season at the time I make it. This is a good mix.

1 large, skinless chicken breast (sliced)
1 pint (drained) Marvelous Mandarin Oranges – divided
3 tablespoons Marvelous Mandarin Orange syrup
3 tablespoons sesame seed
1 tablespoon Chinese five-spice
1 tablespoon minced garlic
1 tablespoon minced fresh ginger root
2 hot red peppers, chopped
1 cup cashew nuts
1/2 cup fresh mushrooms
4 chopped green onions
soy sauce to taste

Stir-fry vegetables until crisp and bright. Thicken with cornstarch, mixed with small amount of water. Cook a few minutes until thickened. Serve over rice, with the other 1/2 pint of drained Marvelous Mandarin Oranges arranged on top.

Recipe Notes

Our Brazen Fruit Vinegarettes

After canning any of our series of pickled fruits, you will have some remaining vinegarette. Bottle it very hot; clean rims of jars and process in boiling water bath for 5 minutes. Remove and cool.

Brazen Fruit Vinegarette Uses and Suggestions:
All of the fruit vinegars can be thickened for glazes. Use straight for salad dressing or mix with olive oil. Good in hot and iced drinks. Good for marinades and stir-fries. Use your imagination!

In Conclusion .....

When is family not always family? The answer to this riddle can be found in the Bible. There, Jesus tells us His family is those who love and obey God's teaching. So you see, sometimes we acquire new family members that are not biologically or legally related to us, but through our common love for Him.

Through an interesting pattern of events years ago, Judy Joy was woven into the fabric that is our family and now is very much a part of us.

Since Judy and I are close in age and often enjoy similar things, our relationship seems more like sisters than just friends.

During the long, hectic summer garden days, we look forward to fish feeding time. Late in the day, while we still have light, Judy gets that sparkle in her eyes and queries, "Do you want to feed the fish now?"

Fish feeding time is a kaleidoscope of sensory stimulation. First, there's the walk to the granary to get the fish food. While there, we stop to respond to the demanding chatter of the ducks and geese as they run to us to see if we've brought them a treat from the gardens. They seem to be trying to best each other, in attempts to get our full attention. Then we have to stop and admire the beautiful new breeds of chickens, freshly hatched just months before. The full colors of their plumage show more each week. Usually we also stop to pet the proud new momma and admire her litter of adorable pink baby pigs. All this and we're just now ready to feed the fish!

The short walk to our beautiful little pond, with its expansive new dock (which goes to the very center and deepest part of the pond) is a seasonal drama, from the wildflowers and beautiful grasses to the ever changing blues, whites, grays, purples and vibrant oranges, reds, peach and pink that paint the expanse of sky laid bare above us like a new book, teasing us to guess the ending in the first chapter. Judy and I walk and talk and laugh and share a love that has stood the test of time – as all true, lasting relationships must.

We cross the little bridge, delighting to the babbling of the tiny brook below, which seems odd yet like a well kept prairie secret. Crossing over, we check on Jared's baby trees and marvel once again at his sheer genius and anointing for life.

We follow the well-worn curving path, ever watchful for an occasional snake, until we reach the dock. The wind plays with us as we walk to the center of the pond, like a wild, free friend. We just stand there for a moment in time, breathing in all the beauty around us.

To the south of the pond is the cozy little log home, to the north is our six generation dwelling; to the west is the little house on the prairie, which rejoices in the patter of our first grandchildren's feet. Interwoven throughout is the ever-constant prairie - - which is restoring itself with a little help from us.

Judy and I speak to the fish, "Come here, little fish. It's feeding time." And they come. We throw out the food and soon the term, "The water seemed to boil with fish," takes on a new meaning. They are beautiful, so graceful. Their bodies reflecting the ebbing rays of the twilight's sun.

We watch as long as we dare. Satisfied, we turn to go back. It's been a good day, a good life – one in which we are not ashamed. We have given back more than we took, and all of nature approves. The kingdom of heaven is at hand.

ORDER FORM

To order additional copies of From Poetry to Pickles, fill out the information below and mail to:

Hearth and Home Publishing
12989 Windy Road
Bucklin, KS 67834

Or call 316-826-3491 to order.

Payment should be made by check, money order, or Visa or Mastercard.

Information on upcoming books by Shirley, including the next three books: Sunlight and Shadows, From a Country Heart, and So You Can't Boil Water?, will also be sent upon request.

Thank you. It's a joy to share with you!

Name: _____
Address: _____
_____
Phone Number: _____

Payment Method: (select one)
❑ Check ❑ Money Order ❑ Visa ❑ Mastercard
Credit Card Number: _____
Expiration Date: _____
Signature: _____

Number of copies ordered: _____ @ $17.95 $ _____
Shipping and Handling: $2.50 (per book) $ _____
    Kansas residents 5.9% Tax: $ _____
                Total: $ _____

Please send information only on upcoming books:
(select one or more).
❑ Sunlight and Shadows (the poetry of a heart)
❑ From a Country Heart (a back-to-basics book of farm life tips)
❑ Heartland Hearth (a country cookbook)

Additional Order Form

To order additional copies of From Poetry to Pickles, fill out the information below and mail to:

Hearth and Home Publishing
12989 Windy Road
Bucklin, KS 67834

Or call 316-826-3491 to order.

Payment should be made by check, money order, or Visa or Mastercard.

Information on upcoming books by Shirley, including the next three books: Sunlight and Shadows, From a Country Heart, and So You Can't Boil Water?, will also be sent upon request.

Thank you. It's a joy to share with you!

Name: _____
Address: _____
_____
Phone Number: _____

Payment Method: (select one)
❏Check   ❏Money Order   ❏Visa   ❏Mastercard
Credit Card Number: _____
Expiration Date: _____
Signature: _____

Number of copies ordered: _____ @ $17.95 $ _____
Shipping and Handling: $2.50 (per book) $ _____
      Kansas residents 5.9% Tax: $ _____
                          Total: $ _____

Please send information only on upcoming books:
(select one or more).
❏Sunlight and Shadows (the poetry of a heart)
❏From a Country Heart (a back-to-basics book of farm life tips)
❏Heartland Hearth (a country cookbook)